ACKN

To myself. I love you. Your courage is inspiring, and I am so proud of you for living your truth. May it be a platform for others. To the Universe, a million thank you is not enough! Thank you for my happiness, peace, peace of mind, healing, forgivingness, understanding, compassion, and empathy.

INTRODUCTION

I chose to be in this world, and, to this end, I choose to be happy. I thought long and hard about whether to share my story. Whether another "here's how hard my life was" would make a difference or help anyone. Then I reminded myself that no matter how many "hard knock life" stories are told none of them are the same. Therefore, each one is needed in order to touch someone who the other stories may not have reached. So, with this in mind, along with a throbbing heart because of my sheer vulnerability in putting pen to paper, I decided to share my own. I attempted to write in sequential order but found that I wanted to complete certain thoughts. Also, everything included is based on real events although, with the passage of time, my memory may have added or omitted certain details. In addition, because some of these topics are inevitably sensitive, I do not mean to tarnish anyone's character. This, however, is my truth—my traumatic life experiences as lived by me with the corresponding emotions.

Chapter 1

As far back as I can remember, my maternal grandmother has always told me that I was a "special child." Without much context or meaning I wasn't sure what to make of this statement. As I became older and started on my proverbial journey of self-discovery I wanted to know more about this phrase and I also wanted to know why I acted the way I did.

Well, I learned at approximately twenty years old that I was aborted.

That is, my mother actually took whatever pill she needed to take in order to terminate my life, but instead "I chose to be in this world" because I remained alive. I'll later get back to how I learned of this key information. Then at thirty-one years old, I learned that later in her pregnancy my mother "thought she was losing me," but yet again "I chose to be in this world" because I remained in the womb full term.

In retrospect, I realized that I endured two traumatic experiences before I was truly ever born into this world. Two traumatic experiences that nonetheless left an imprint on my infantile brain and barely existent nervous system. Yet, one thing I know for sure is that from the time I was in the womb I knew there was something greater for which to live. Now, after learning of these tragic events, my maternal grandmother's statement made absolute sense. I defied all odds that were stacked against me and fought not once but twice because my life really depended on it.

Then on August 2, 1988, on a bed in a small house in Montego Bay, Jamaica the little fighter was born. Now surely, because I had experienced significant trauma before birth, my actual life was destined to be easier right? Not quite.

Chapter 2

Apparently, when my mother was in labor with me my father did not believe she was about to deliver. So, instead of coming to take my mother to the hospital, she did not know how to drive, my mother remained at home. No doctor, no nurse, no midwife. Just my maternal grandmother to fill those roles—without any formal training.

For context, my parents were hot in love when I was conceived, but they were not in a stable relationship by the time I arrived. At the time of my birth, my dad was twenty years old, young, and just starting out his career as a newly minted police officer in Montego Bay. My mother was also young, eighteen years old, now a mother of two, having my brother at fifteen years old, and a cosmetologist working hard to make ends meet. My father wanted to enjoy the perks of his budding career and authority while my mother wanted him to become a committed family man. Needless to say, tensions grew high between the two and my father went on his way after I was born. The story is that my father was in my life until I was two years old, but naturally I have no memory of this.

With only one parent financially supporting me, my mother went back to work as a cosmetologist almost immediately after giving birth in order to provide for her two kids. She also had to help out my maternal grandmother with bills around the house. As you can imagine, I suffered deeply for this from infancy into childhood because now not only did I lack a loving father around I also lacked the constant care and attention of my primary caregiver—albeit because she "had to put food on the table." Thus, although my mother "was around" more than my dad, I felt like she was barely there to care for me.

I don't recall "meeting" my dad until I was eight years old, which during this same meeting I also learned that I had a four-year-old sister. Because my newly discovered sister accompanied my dad, I was bewildered about the reason for the visit. On one hand I wondered if he visited because he loved and missed me while on the other, I wondered whether he visited simply to introduce me to his other daughter. And, as you can imagine, my "first time meeting my dad" I realized I now had to share his love and affection with another.

The problem for me was that she appeared to already have it because she arrived with him hand in hand.

From the time I met him at eight years old, I don't remember spending much time with him again until I was about ten when I spent my first summer with him in Kingston. In between that time, there were a lot of broken promises, wishful thinking, and unfulfilled hopes. He would constantly reassure me that he was coming to visit, or that he was sending money, or that he was buying a gift especially for me. But none of these ever came to fruition. I was constantly disappointed yet every time he would make a new promise, I would steadfastly hang on to his every word. I somehow learned to just not get my hopes up any longer, to not expect anything good from anyone, and instead doubt when someone says he or she will do something. As you can imagine I grew very distrusting of people as I got older—especially of men and with a particular emphasis on men I dated.

As you can also imagine, growing up without a father figure affected me greatly. I lacked that parent showing me love; I lacked him teaching me, through his actions towards my mother, how a man should love a woman. I did not learn how beautiful I was, how special I was, how loved I was, or how significant I was from the person who should have been the most important male in my life. I felt like I was deprived of the male attention I needed.

Instead, in the absence of my father, I remember having a lot of "uncles." These men were not related to me in any way except they were "friends" of my mother. I had to call them uncle because they were too old for me to address them by first name, and they were not my dad so I could not refer to them as such. I always thought these uncles came in and out like a revolving door. From what I recall, as a young girl I did not like seeing so many men come and go. As you can imagine, I could never get fully attached to any of these men because they would be here today and gone tomorrow. I also thought it was disgusting that so many men could have been having intimate relations with my mother. Of course, I could never express these sentiments to my mother. Yet another event that negatively impacted me. Seeing this pattern, I vowed to myself that I would never ever date so many men, which subconsciously may have also been a reason I stayed in the relationships discussed later.

So, having fought to come into this world, I then encounter what I can imagine registered as neglect from my mother and father as well as inconsistency with any other paternal figures. Not only that, as I got older I remember my mother and maternal grandmother constantly berating my father and making remarks such as "you don't have a father," or "that worthless father of yours" and much worse. Every bit of anger and rage particularly from my mother and maternal grandmother, as a result of my dad's absence, was conveyed directly to me. These statements and more of a similar tone were made repeatedly.

The problem with these statements especially for a young child, however, is that a young child idolizes his/her parent even if the parent is in fact a disappointment. I believe parents lose sight of the fact that disparaging remarks made about another parent in front of a child equally hurts and bruises the child. Repeated disparaging remarks translates to repeated hurt of a child. I had been trapped in the middle of these verbal grenades pelted at my dad for years into adulthood. (One such time, while in undergraduate school, I called my dad to inform him about yet another verbal attack and to ask if the allegations by my mother were true, he instead pelted his own verbal grenade against her and that is how I learned of her abortion while I was in the womb.)

Now, I fought for my life twice while in the womb. Outside of the womb, I felt neglected and attacked because my father (whom I loved in spite of his absence) was being attacked. But I chose to be in this world, and I think subconsciously (and unknowingly) this fighter spirit, this proclaimed "special child" knew to persevere.

Chapter 3

As I got older and my ability to perceive strengthened, I would describe my mother as becoming angrier and angrier. I can remember her always arguing with someone, shouting loud enough for the entire neighborhood to hear, and always fighting with some woman or another. I have very little stories of my mother and I spending quality time together. I have just as few stories of my extended family including my mother, brother, maternal grandmother, aunt, and two cousins participating in any type of family bonding events. I remember receiving beatings frequently from my mother for what I recall being "no reason at all." Now, I'm sure if you ask kids their opinion on beatings, most would say they were "good kids" and/or should not have been beaten. But I aspire to be as unbiased as possible on the issue.

See, growing up I excelled academically. I also enjoyed dancing and watching tv in the spare time I was allotted when not doing homework or doing "extra lessons" to get ahead of my classmates. I rarely got myself "into trouble" and had only one really good friend in the neighborhood with whom I often played. For the most part, I went to school and came home. For some reason, however, I felt like my mother would find a reason to beat me. And I recall these beatings being frequent and at times cruel. I remember distinctively her slapping me across the face so hard she drew blood. Why? I believe it was because she told me to do the dishes and I said it wasn't fair because it was my brother's week to do the dishes. I also remember, if she were upset at me for something, she would wait for me to come home and do everything as normal. I would then shower and as I was exiting, she would beat me while I was still dripping wet so the licks could "sting more." I would be covered in welts. Just imagine how heightened my sensory responses were at not knowing when I would have done something to upset her and when I would suffer the same fate.

I remember another occasion where she came home late one night. I was sleeping and she must have taken particular notice that my hair was wrapped as if protecting it from getting messed up while I slept. She woke me up in the middle of the night, knowing I had to get to school early the next morning, and asked me why my hair was wrapped up. I told her my friend did my hair since she (my mom) was at work all day and couldn't do it. She (my mom) beat me that night because she told me "not to let anybody, especially that girl, 'play' in my hair." She also told me to stay up and take it out. I stayed up crying into the late morning while taking out my braids. My mother went to sleep. I woke the next morning knocking on her door to ask her to do my hair, since I had to undo my previous hairstyle, but there was no answer. So, my hair was nicely done, but I was forced to take it out. I instead had to wear a makeshift hairstyle to school that day simply to please my mother and one of her rages.

These are just a few of what I can recall. Although I am certain there were more instances of unreasonable corporal punishment. My memory may be a bit distorted because of the passage of time, but emotions and imprints on the nervous system remain. And, if there's one thing I remember from growing up it's the lingering feeling of being unloved. I felt like my mother hated me, and she took out her anger on me. As I alluded to earlier, I excelled academically but I do not recall my mother ever telling me good job. Not when I received a passing mark. Not when I received a really high score on a test. Not when I placed first in a class. Not when I placed in the top three of my classes. I felt like neither I nor my achievements were good enough in her eyes. As I grew older, I began thinking maybe she took out the anger she fostered towards my father on me.

Again, only a small child and I have already experienced so much. While in the womb I had to fight twice for my life. Once born into the world, I felt neglected, attacked because my father was constantly attacked, unloved, not good enough, and physically abused by my mother. But, this "special child" was going to keep pushing for survival.

Chapter 4

Then, I recall being molested by my older brother. I don't know how old I was or how old he was. I do know we are three years apart. I suppose that I must have been between toddler and infant age because I think otherwise, I would have had a better recollection of the details. Also, it had to have been before I was twelve years old because I already moved away by then. I don't recall how many times or how often, but I do know that it happened. I distinctively remember one Saturday we were on a bed and I was on top of him. Neither of us had on any bottoms.

I remember an adult walking in, seeing us, and exclaiming something to the effect of what's going on. I remember feeling somewhat relieved because I thought he would get in trouble. However, I don't recall anything ever coming of the incident. I don't even recall anyone asking me if I were okay or anyone taking me to get checked out by a doctor. All I remember is retreating in silence like nothing ever happened—never to mention the incident or any other similar incidents to anyone, ever. I felt ashamed, dirty, and stained. I remained in silence for a very long time.

I was silent until I was twenty-seven years old. After all those years, why then? Well, I planned to return to Jamaica with one of my closest friends for the first time since I left at the age of thirteen. Not only that, but I was staying with my brother, alone, for the first portion of my trip. By this time, I had not seen my brother in about fifteen years. I never rationalized why I had not tried to see my brother in so long or why not visiting didn't seem to trouble me. But, with this trip, it all made sense. I started feeling uneasy and nervous as the travel date approached. I could not put a finger on why these emotions were stirring, but then memories of that fateful Saturday flooded in my mind. Him making a circle and inserting his finger "in and out" also kept replaying in my mind as if he were secretly making advances towards me.

I finally shared the information with my friend and her first response was whether I wanted to instead stay with her and her family for the entire trip. As the Universe would have it, however, I decided to stay with my brother because "I wanted to address the issue." But, during that time, I was unable to address it. For the few days I stayed by him, we slept on his one full-sized mattress and I laid awake every night fearful. The thought kept rushing back to me and I didn't have the courage to tell him that I remembered what occurred at least that one Saturday. I never mentioned anything, just like when I was younger, and I never dared mention the incident ever again to anyone. Instead, I called my friend and asked her to come pick me up early from my brother's place.

Although I did not address the issue as I thought I would, I believe the

Universe accomplished its goal, which was to bring a very important feeling and emotion to the forefront of my mind after being locked away for so long. This was just the warmup, however, because the Universe was not done releasing me of this trauma.

Fast forward to twenty-eight years old when I was still fresh off the tail end of a breakup that sent me into a tailspin of feeling unloved, unworthy, and undeserving. I went to spend some time with my maternal grandmother and step-grandfather. At some point, my maternal grandmother and I were watching an episode of "Iyanla Vanzant's Fix My Life." I believe the angry black woman storyline was being aired wherein a lady was recapping the sexual abuse she suffered at the hand of her stepfather. I was so moved I began crying uncontrollably. Because my emotions were so strong, my grandmother started to inquire as to the root cause, and I accused her of already knowing.

She stated that she had no idea of what I was referring, and I told her she did because she walked in on us when we were younger. She denied my accusation. I then brought myself to tell her about my brother molesting me. Her initial response was "what did I do to make him do that to me." Then she followed up by saying it was not her who walked in. I eventually found out it was my mother who had walked in on that fateful Saturday. My mother. I don't recall her scolding him. I don't recall her hugging me. I don't recall her asking me if I were okay or for any details. I recall just utter silence and disregard as if nothing happened.

When I addressed my mother, she told me I was lying about the sexual abuse occurring more than once because "she had spoken to him about it at the time and he said it was only once." So, she at least confirmed that it occurred, but at the same time I realized she had a conversation with my brother. The person I felt wronged me and deserved rightful repercussions, she comforted. Yet, as her daughter—the one who felt victimized—she didn't speak with me. It's as if at twenty-eight years old I received reassurance that my feeling of being unloved as a child was accurate.

Can you imagine? I fought twice to stay alive. I was eager to come into this world! But I was met with feeling attacked, neglected, unloved, unworthy, undeserving, insignificant, and not good enough. I experienced physical abuse and sexual abuse. But, as special as I was, surely, I had to make it in this life. No way this would be this fighter's story.

Chapter 5

Growing up, I felt like I was mostly invisible—except academically. I buried my head in my books and continued to excel. I was popular amongst my primary school classmates and even found time to participate in my school's makeshift netball and poetry teams. Then, at almost twelve years old, a daunting day came upon me. My father arrived in his black SUV and started loading up stuffed animals and bags in the back. When he arrived, I thought this was just one of his random drop-ins until another year or two. So, I naively continued playing outside with a cousin of mine and my friend—the same friend who did my hair, which prompted my beating. Unbeknownst to me, while I was completing my last year of primary school, my parents seemed to put their rift aside so that a master plan could unfold.

After he finished packing the items into the vehicle, my dad turned to me and said something to the effect of "alright we're leaving now." Puzzled and confused I had no idea what he meant. Granted, I figured I was going off to high school in Kingston. At this time in Jamaica, once a student reached the final grade of primary school—the 6th grade—he or she would choose his or her top three high schools and then take a mandatory "Common Entrance Exam." Successful passage of the exam would result in that student attending one of his or her chosen schools. In my case, however, I should add that my school selections did not actually take into consideration my choices. All I knew was, the schools chosen on my behalf were all located in Kingston. That was the extent of my knowledge. I do not recall anyone having a conversation with me to really explain that I would be moving or when.

All I can remember from the day I moved away with my dad is entering the vehicle and crying for what felt like the entire drive from Montego Bay to Portmore. All I could think of was how I never got to say goodbye to my friends, some of whom I have been in the same class with since the first grade. At the time, I felt agony so deep I thought it was unbearable. I had to have cried for months because of this great loss that I felt as an eleven-soon-to-be-twelve-year-old girl. Because a move is usually a decision made by the adults in a household for varying reasons, most adults don't stop to consider how devastating and traumatic a change in environment can be on a child. It really is mind and life altering especially if the child is in the dark about the whole thing.

Then, the biggest shocker came as the master plan unfolded. Not long after I went to live with my dad, my mom called "to check on me and make sure I was alright." During the conversation she casually mentioned that she was in England. England!

Shock and sadness instantly overcame me. Although growing up I felt unloved and treated unfairly by her—she was still my mother. I had no idea she would leave for another country and the biggest blow—she told my brother everything about her departure and kept me in the dark.

As you can imagine, the hurt and pain just piled on to my poor little nervous system. Not only did I now have imprints from fighting to stay alive twice. I suffered feeling neglected, attacked, unloved, unworthy, insignificant, not good enough, abandoned, betrayed, and deceived. In addition, I experienced physical and sexual abuse. At this point, there's no more that this "special child" could experience right? Wrong again.

After the agony subsided and I internalized my mother's disappearance, I had gotten quite used to finally having my dad in my life. I finally felt like he loved me. I finally began feeling like I was deserving. Yet, I don't recall my dad ever telling me I was beautiful. I don't recall him hugging me just because. Outside of living together, we really didn't spend much time together. He never taught me how to ride a bike or took me to the park to spend quality time. We seemed to just simply share the same space while I lived with him. I remember going to his office after school one day, and it's as if he had an epiphany because as I waited for him to finish reviewing a stack of documents, he turned to me and said, "you know I didn't realize I loved you this much." At first, I was happy with his statement and responded with a beaming smile. Then, I lowered my head as my brain started to wonder whether he was just realizing he loved me or whether he never loved me fully prior to this moment. I could no longer find the joy in his statement.

Nonetheless, I was still joyous that I finally had him in my life, and I was in his. It's like once I began living with him all of his failures and disappointments were erased. Until the day he introduced me to his mistress. I had never been intricately involved in or witnessed an affair; I had only ever heard reference of the act in songs or passerby conversations amongst adults. So, I was distraught when it became real life. I had never imagined my father as a cheater. See, my dad dated his then girlfriend for about seven years by the time I went to live with him. She never tried to be my mother but instead tried to be the best stepmother to me that she could. I was comfortable with her and took a liking to her.

Then, one day when my dad picked me up after school he stopped by an unfamiliar building and told me he was picking up a friend from work as well. It went from picking up this friend occasionally to picking her up regularly. Then, before I knew it, my stepmother left to work in the [United]

States for a few months. Not sooner than the day she left, the mistress packed her bags and began staying in my father's house. Can you imagine my confusion? I felt disgusted, hurt, angry, and deceived. Worst of all, I could not express to him my displeasure with him and his actions. I had to remain quiet and carry on as if his actions were right or as if I condoned them. So, I became mute. I barely spoke to my dad and I certainly would not address the mistress. I did not eat the food when she cooked. I did not pretend to be happy. I would sit at the dinner table in silence while the two would be enjoying their meal until I would finally ask to go to my room or my father would send there. At one point I believe she said something to the effect that I hated her but in honesty I did because her actions were wrong—and so were his. I could not understand how she could carry on with a man that's not hers and how my father could happily carry on with another woman knowing that he had a girlfriend.

The mistress stayed at the house up until the day my stepmother returned from her seasonal job in the States. She (the mistress) left in the morning and by the afternoon my dad and I were decorating the house and blowing up balloons to welcome my stepmother back home. When my stepmom arrived at the house my dad's first statement was "I missed you so much, honey." I couldn't believe my ears! I wanted to throw up! Right then and there I wanted to call him a liar and tell her everything, but I remained silent. I remained silent because I was trapped. I felt like I wanted to do the "right thing" by telling the truth but incidentally betraying my father who I loved. On the other hand, because he was my father and I loved him, I also wanted to keep his secret and protect him.

It's as if this robbed me of any little innocence I had left. My youth, my belief in relationships, and my faith in honest loyal men were all shattered. I mean, as a young girl, when you think of an ideal man you tend to think of your father. Here, I had an inconsistent father who came in and out of my life, made false promises, and now cheated. What a life for this "special child." I can imagine and see how fearful I was of dating as I got older. When I was about twenty-three or twenty-four, I mentioned this incident to my dad and I explained how crushing it was for me and how much of a negative impact it had on me growing up. Yet my father's response was "baby that was the most confused I have ever been in my life." Not once did he apologize. Not once did he own up to the role he played in my confusion and pain witnessing what I had as a young girl. Instead, he made it about himself and justified his behavior.

Chapter 6

After the first year living with my dad, I visited one of my aunts in the country during the summer of my thirteenth birthday. Unbeknownst to me, however, was how friendly towards me her husband would become. He tended to hug me a little too long when my aunt was not around or to caress the outer shape of my still developing body while hugging me. I wanted to say something to my aunt, but I could not. Of course, at the time, not linking my inability to speak with the molestation I experienced earlier in my already very young life. I remember towards the end of my visit when we went to the beach and knowing I could not swim, he offered to help "teach me." Although hesitant because of his earlier advances, I innocently accepted the offer because I was still a child eager to have child-like experiences such as learning how to swim. I guess I should have known better because his hand was on my vagina the entire time he was "teaching how to swim." Although he never inserted any of fingers, his actions were repulsively inappropriate, and I felt violated. I was so disappointed in myself for trusting him to do the right thing.

So, here I am, thirteen years old, I went back to my dad's and never uttered a word. I just continued keeping on like this "special child" knew how. Then shortly into the start of my school year another blow. My dad sat me down to tell me he quit his job and decided to move to the [United] States because he was fed up. As I listened, I waited patiently to hear how much consideration he had for me in making his decision. I waited eagerly to hear the rest of his plan, but none of it included me moving with him. Instead, he reassured me that I would stay with my stepmom and her mother.

Can you imagine! Here I was now pawned off by both of my parents.

Abandoned by both. Not good enough for either of them to take me with them. Not worthy or deserving enough for either of them to make sure I was safe. None of my parents wanted to stick around and care for me. I was distraught! I was unspeakably broken in so many ways it was unimaginable. But the fighting spirit remained. I kept on keeping on. I tried to remain in good spirits and focus on what I had.

I lived with my stepmom for a few months. I can't recall what transpired whether she and my dad ended their relationship or whether my maternal grandmother and mother had an issue with me living with my stepmom. But, within a few months I ended up being shuffled to live with one of my dad's sisters. I felt so disrupted. I was unsettled with no structure, no stability, no control over my life as it unfolded. I felt like I could never breathe a sigh of relief or sit back and trust that I would have some normalcy. I grew to always anticipate the next interruption, the next change, the next disappointment. If something were going "too good," it's as if I couldn't fully enjoy because I was looking over my shoulder for the next let down.

Although I am grateful my aunt obliged and I was staying with family, moving in with my aunt meant that I was intruding on a family of four who rented one room in a two- or three-bedroom house. My aunt and her three children all shared one bed but there was a pull-out bed hidden in a couch on which my girl cousin and I would sleep. At this point, I believe my mother and maternal grandmother would send money to ensure I would have food and personal toiletries. And, while I was grateful for the sustenance, I felt alone in my circumstance. I would also become overwhelmed with guilt knowing that I would go to school with adequate bus fare and lunch money while my cousins would maybe have bus fare to get to school—without much else. I remember being so conscientious of my new "family struggle" that I would reuse a sanitary napkin for more than one day if it only had little body fluid. I didn't want to be a burden in asking for additional money.

At thirteen, I was already walking around with serious emotional trauma, which, for the most part, were never addressed. How could I be such a "special child" when life just kept hitting me from every angle? How could I be such a "special child" when my own parents didn't seem to want me? How could I be such a "special child" when it seemed no one was there to protect me. As you can fathom, I can probably go on and on down the rabbit hole of questions I am sure I had as a child. But I will not belabor that point. I will say that even when I was stuck in the dark hole of my emotions, I still knew I was meant for greater in this life, so I kept on keeping on.

Chapter 7

I eventually relocated to the [United] States several months after my dad left me. Not to live with him, but instead to live with my maternal grandmother and step-grandfather. It seemed that my dad had no intentions of bringing me to live with him any time soon, so my maternal grandmother and step-grandfather intervened. And, while I was, and still am, grateful for all they did, there was still a void because they were not my parents. The ones who should have loved, protected, and provided for me unconditionally failed me. Instead, I am now living with my adopted parents—although still members of my family. And to top it off, I am living in a new country with different expectations and customs but harboring the same old emotional trauma. Undeniably, this move was yet another disruption in my life. Stability, steadiness, and normalcy to me all seemed like foreign states of being.

The pattern of constant interruption left me on edge wondering and anticipating when the next life altering interference may occur. Although, this marital, two-parent household was the closest I would get to normalcy during the remainder of my rearing years, which in and of itself says a lot because my home life here was far from normal.

The next traumatic occurrence took place about one year after moving. I remember an incident at fourteen years old. I was talking on the phone with a schoolmate and my step-grandfather apparently needed to use the phone. There was only one line in the house at the time so if someone were using the phone another was prevented from using it. My step-grandfather picked up one of the phones and, in a very aggressive and short tone, he announced that I need to get off the phone because he needs to use it. Well, I guess I wasn't off the phone fast enough because as I was about to hang up the phone he rushed into my room and grabbed the phone receiver out of my hand yelling "Didn't I tell you to get off the phone." Enraged, as I was starting to recognize anger as my base emotion due to all of the unaddressed trauma I had endured, I shouted that I was getting off the phone. The audacity of me responding to him in that matter seemed to anger him even more because he grabbed me by the throat until I elevated off the ground. My step-grandfather was fifty-four years old at the time. He choked me as if I was a full aged man—not even a woman. I immediately started crying.

I called my grandmother to tell her what happened and all she said was "it's okay Sherri-Ann." She did not say let me talk to him. She did not say I'll handle it when he comes to get me from work later. Nothing. I then called one of my maternal uncles who simply said, "that's how he gets Sherri-Ann he has a problem." I then called one of my maternal aunts who said, "don't worry about it Sherri-Ann he's not going to change." Then, when my grandmother came home. The house was silent. Not a sound. I don't even recall her comforting me. I felt like no one rescued me, no one made sure I was okay. Even worse for me, no one admonished him. He suffered no repercussions; he was not "punished for his behavior." Eerily, I felt as helpless as I imagine I did when my mother caught my brother molesting me and did nothing to ensure I was safe or to punish him. Instead, the silence just allowed the guilt to transfer to me. Some special child, right? Thereafter, I continued adjusting to this country and my new life as best I knew how. My grandfather would constantly be in one of his moods and I as well as my grandmother was just supposed to stay clear because he could overact at any time. My state of uneasiness remained. Also, I learned of his cheating ways and just as quickly as he would cheat,

I would be enraged for my grandmother, and she would silently acquiesce his actions and carry on as if nothing ever happened. Then there were times I would hear them arguing and then a slap would ring out so loud that I would come running from the room raging. My grandmother would just stand there without defending herself. I began to dislike this "normal set up" and began questioning unions and relationships as a whole because to me they all seemed miserable.

All of this and I subconsciously maintained my level of happiness and kindness. Consciously, however, I was still broken inside.

I had my first real boyfriend at fifteen years old. With all my experience, however, I was almost bound to have a dysfunctional relationship. I started on an unhealthy cycle of "break up to make up." My ex-boyfriend and I dated for about a year and a half. Like most normal "puppy love" high school relationships, however, I decided I no longer wanted to be in a relationship with him. But, of course, what was normal about my life at this point? When I first broke up with him, he ran away from home and threatened to take his life. He would send cryptic text messages to my cell phone and/or his family's cell phones, which would then lead to me or them calling him incessantly. Once he would answer the phone, I would then either talk or cry with him over the phone all night. If he did not answer the phone, I would frantically call him none stop to no avail and was left in fear thinking the worse.

The saga carried on for months and I became somewhat of a strategist. At about seventeen years old, here I was constantly on edge defusing life threatening situations while most teens were going to the movies. I ultimately was forced to make up with him just to ensure his safe return home. When he did return home and hugged me, because he was "so happy to have me back," I felt depleted and empty. I felt like I gave up my being just so his would remain. I felt deceitful because I was not being true to myself or him. Again, I felt insignificant because my needs and wants did not matter in the situation. I had to do what would make others happy. Once I felt comfortable enough with him reintegrating back into school and his family, I broke it off with him again. At this point, high school administration placed me on a "suicidal/homicidal watch."

This is when things took a strange turn—because again what was normal in my life. Although at school I was on a high alert watch, my ex-boyfriend would regularly come over to my house, without my invitation, and berate me. How would he get in you wonder? Well, my grandmother would appease him. She allowed him into the house and to my room door on a regular basis to yell at me and pass remarks such as "I am a whore," "I only broke up with him so I can f--k other boys in school," "My name is written all over the bathrooms and desks," "I would not find anyone better than him," or "I was making the biggest mistake of my life." Mind you, I believe I was still a virgin at this point i.e. I don't even think he and I even had sex yet. I was in the top 5% of my class, and I kept busy on three sports teams and several organizations. I had no time or desire to be this person he described. My grandmother could hear all of his remarks and allowed his actions.

I feared for my life and avoided this boy every possible chance I got, but my grandmother would casually allow him into the house to demean me. On some nights, I would even hear him at my window crying and/or begging me to let him inside. It got to the point where I slept on the floor by the door because I was scared if he should break the window. During this period, I retreated to being as quiet as I was when I was a small child and felt like no one came to my defense or took my feelings into consideration. I barely ate any of the food my grandparents cooked, and I barely left my room when we were all in the house at the same time. It was more like a hunger strike than anything else. And, when I was home alone, I would nibble on light snacks so there was no indication that I had eaten anything. This was my cry out for things to stop, similar to when I lived with my dad, but just like then I don't remember my grandparents ever intervening or having a conversation with me to make sure I was okay.

The night of my senior prom, I missed most of the actual dance and have zero pictures to commemorate the evening. Why? Well, I ended up attending prom with another classmate and my ex-boyfriend barged into my home fully dressed in formal attire as my date and I were gearing up for photos. He (my ex-boyfriend) was yelling obscenities and alleging that I ruined his life. All I recall is that my step-grandfather threw a punch, the police were called, and I ended up being almost two hours late to prom. Once I arrived at prom, I was anxious and on high alert because my ex-boyfriend appeared to be headed to prom as well. I could barely enjoy the music or my friends. Then, sure enough, my friends began to surround me as we danced, and they informed me that he (my ex-boyfriend) arrived.

I spent the remainder of the night checking over my shoulders and mainly dancing in between a circle of my friends.

All of that and I went back to dating this fellow for an additional two years or so. Talk about trauma on top of trauma. Now this became my standard for relationships. Surely, this must be what a healthy relationship is like right? All couples must fight constantly, become enraged, are life threatening, and break up to make up right? In addition, from what I witnessed from my dad and step-grandfather, all men lie, cheat, are physically abusive, and ticking time bombs. As you can imagine, with a life of unresolved traumatic events, my next relationship was not the healthiest either.

Chapter 8

I began dating my next boyfriend at about twenty years old. I was a junior in college and from the outside looking in I had it all together. Again, I knew how to keep on keeping on. I did so well at it that apparently most everyone who knew of me in college thought I had "the perfect life," although what I had experienced was the furthest from it. In this relationship, I carried over the breakup to make up cycle, but I added another layer. I would now shut down if I felt like he was getting too close to me emotionally. For that matter, around this time in my life, that was my defense mechanism if anyone were getting too close to me. During one of the break up to make up cycles, I was staying at his apartment. For whatever reason I was upset and decided to emotionally shut down. I would not speak to him. A few days went by where I gave him the cold shoulder and closed myself off sexually. I had done this many times before, sometimes for days, weeks, or even months at a time. But he decided enough was enough. This time around, he decided I would speak.

He dragged me out of the bed by one foot and said we needed to talk. I got dressed and went out into the living room. Tensions were high. I had nothing to say and he wanted everything to be said. I don't recall all the details, but I said I was leaving. One problem. He was standing in my way somewhat obstructing the door. So, I squeezed by him to make my exit. Apparently, I grazed him as I was making my way out so with full force and both arms, he shoved me into the neighboring door. The push was so forceful that the door flung open. The neighbor ran downstairs to find out what the noise was, but I was already off the ground and back in my ex-boyfriend's apartment just from sheer disbelief and embarrassment. My ex-boyfriend immediately pleaded and begged me not to tell anyone as I grabbed my phone. I called my dad crying and telling him what I had just experienced. Instantly, it was as if something triggered in my ex-boyfriend and he stopped pleading and became enraged. He started yelling my name loud enough for the entire neighborhood to hear. He shouted remarks such as "I need to get out of his place," "I am dead to him," "I am nothing to him" etc. and he proceeded to take all of my clothes and shoes from his closet and throw them outside on the ground.

Although this was not the first time he put his hands on me, this was the first time I equated it to being hit. Prior to this incident, he had grabbed me, picked me up into the air, and shaken me about twice before. So, it was a like a build up to domestic violence, but all domestic violence, nonetheless. I felt low, distraught, and confused. Yet, I went back to him and we continued on the make up to break up cycle for a few years later—thankfully with no more physical incidents.

And, although having been "aborted" myself, I ended up having two abortions while still dating him—of which he only knew about one for a very long time. Anyone who decides to have an abortion will attest that the decision is a painful one. But, knowing I myself was "aborted" made my decisions all the more soul shattering. Psychologically, I was shaken up. I honestly only dared rationalizing my decisions for a split second before simply becoming numb to the whole experience because I feared that I was betraying myself. I clearly needed to address the impact of my decisions, but again I just became mute as if to erase their occurrence.

At this point, I had lived through so many experiences that undeniably shaped my outlook on life and myself. From the outside I appeared well, but internally I was covered with emotional and mental sores. Even with these blemishes, however, I continued to fight. I continued to keep on keeping on. The little spirit in me, the one my maternal grandmother referenced kept me—although to it I was not yet awaken.

Chapter 9

I should mention, the fighter spirit kept me so well that I continued to excel academically. I made it all the way to law school. So, at this point, I was about twenty-four years old, in my second year of my law studies and battling with emotional turmoil. Although I knew I lived through some mess, I never really acknowledged them as being traumatic. I also did not dare search the depths of my soul for answers. I just realized that my base reaction had morphed into anger and I did not like it. I was tired of the anger; I was tired of the pain; I was tired of the rage. I still had not connected any of these emotions to my many experiences from the past.

Then one day I prayed a prayer. I asked God to take away my anger, to break my chains, and to free me. I honestly believe the Universe was just waiting on me to finally acknowledge my pain. As soon as I said my prayer, instantaneously a friend with whom I was upset for about two years called me out of nowhere to smooth things over. Right there a bit of anger chipped away, and I felt a warmth beaming from the inside. Alas, the special child within me awakened. The heightened compassion I possessed since I was a child strengthened again. It never escaped me, but it hung on for dear life as I experienced pain after pain. And from that moment on, even as I continued working through my issues and experienced more heartbreaks and disappointments in my life, I walked around with an inexplicable happiness.

At twenty-eight years old, after a breakup that again sent me spiraling down the hole of feeling unworthy and undeserving the Universe, in the form of a friend, recommended that I read a book on attachment theories. As insignificant as this recommendation probably was to my friend, this really was the Universe setting me on my way to fully awakening the special child within—the fighter. I read the book and certain emotions within me started making sense. I finally began to correlate why I reacted with those particular emotions after every breakup. That is, the emotions I felt as a child when my parents abandoned me, were the same emotions that would manifest after a break-up and I felt like my partner abandoned me.

Quickly thereafter I received another recommendation and read another book—The Power of Now, then another recommendation and read another book—The Power of the Subconscious Mind, and another recommendation then another book—Change Your Thoughts, Change Your Life. And, before I knew it, I read many more books and discovered many more philosophies. But the principles that kept me during and after my years of trauma, those unsaid principles by which I seemingly lived, were all placed before me at just the right time by the powers of the Universe. I started to really understand that we are not our circumstances and even with the hardest tragedies everything in life happens as it should.

As difficult as it may be to accept, everything that happens is the best possible thing that could happen because everything will always work out for your favor. If you believe it!

I realized that, irrespective of all that I have been through in life, life is a gift and should be lived with the ever-present joy of receiving said gift. And, from then on out, I chose happiness. Honestly, I chose happiness because it really is the selfish thing to do. It is the easiest way to heal yourself.

Choosing happiness is also the easiest way to take away power and control from the traumatic events that haunt you. It is the best way to not just survive but thrive.

There is no formula to choosing happiness. There is no right or wrong way to do it. There is no magic combination.

Choosing happiness really encompasses finding something to be happy about every day you are alive. It is understanding that you have experienced disappointment in life. In spite of, however, you choose to acknowledge these disappointments and live a joyous life. You do not allow your experiences to keep you stagnant, angry, resentful, depressed, or bitter.

For me, as mentioned earlier, I prayed specific prayers requesting healing. I read numerous books then I put my lessons into action. I started with forgiveness. I made my long laundry list of all who I thought wronged me. And, one by one, I forgave them all in my mind and in my soul. I also forgave myself for all the hurt I caused others. Then, I became more compassionate. I empathized with them all and imagined what struggles they may have been facing at the time of their "wrongdoing" against me. Next, I refined my peace (and peace of mind) in order to not be easily moved or offended by another. I also released any and all control I attempted to exert over others and circumstances because I now truly understood that I am merely a vessel while the God is in control.

I believed in my heart that I was healed. Then, at thirty years old, I dated a thirty-six year old man who was not only mentally and emotionally immature but also emotionally unavailable.

No matter what I said or did there was just no getting through to him. During and towards the tail end of the relationship, I continuously took inventory of myself because I did not like some of my actions, reactions, and responses. As you can imagine, because I believed I was truly healed, I questioned why I attracted this type of person as a partner. I wondered why I continued to tolerate some of his actions. I also wanted to know why I kept trying to make this unhealthy relationship work. I was very confused, but the Universe's purpose was clear. For one, the relationship showed me exactly how I was during my previous relationships—especially during college. It also showed me how far I have come on my journey of mental and emotional healing. Additionally, had it not been for this relationship, I probably would not have taken additional inventory of myself. I would not have read the exact books I needed during that time to trigger further healing, and I probably would not have gone to therapy. Most importantly, I probably would not have finally been propelled to sit down and write this book, which I firmly believe was the final step to my healing.

In any event, to make sure that I was truly healed, I started going to therapy. I wanted from a professional either reassurance of my healing or assistance towards my healing. I truly wanted to make sure I wasn't still harboring hurt and attracting more hurt/trauma into my life. So, I ended up in the office of a psychotherapist. Not thinking anything of it, I continued with the initial evaluations and performed numerous psychoanalytical tests. These tests included the archetypical ones we've seen in movies i.e. look at this paint splat and tell me what you see. To my comfort, the therapist told me there was no indication that I suffered from any mental illness i.e. I was "normal." Not just any normal, confident, secure, sure of myself, self-sufficient with a positive outlook, assertive, and high functioning. I was so grateful to the Universe for my healing, and for bringing me right into the psychotherapist's chair so that I would stop questioning who I am.

I do believe that I always possessed these characteristics even when I was younger and experiencing turmoil. I am certain anyone who has known me for several years would describe me as being happy, kind, sensitive to others, nonjudgmental, and resolute in my compassion towards others. I now realize that even when I was deep in my own mess the principles the Universe showed me later in my life were present in me since before I could recognize them. I would read one book after another and completely feel like I truly lived those principles on a daily basis. That is what I believe my maternal grandmother saw in me when she dubbed me a special child. That is what the Universe wanted me to see in myself. I can now agree that yes, I am that special child. I fought for my life twice while in the womb. I suffered physical abuse; sexual abuse; emotional abuse; domestic violence. I experienced neglect; abandonment; manipulation; unloving, insignificant, and unworthy ideation; deception; turmoil; inconsistency; unpredictability; and a myriad of other heartbreaking feelings. But despite it all, I have life so I will continue to choose happiness again and again.

If I can choose happiness so can you! You may have experienced more than I have, or you may have experienced less. I do not write to compare battle stories. Instead, I merely hope to shine a light on the fact that we are all perfectly imperfect human beings. And I especially want to shine this light in communities where it is taboo to bring attention to certain truths. We were born into this world for a reason greater than ourselves so while here we should make the best of it. Let go of hurt, let go of pain, and live for the joy in each day because your life depends on it.

I'll end with a few quotes by Rumi that helped me on my journey of healing:

"Learn the alchemy true human beings know. The moment you accept what troubles you've been given, the door will open."

"The cure for pain is in the pain."

"The pains you feel are messengers. Listen to them."

"Be silent, only the hand of God can remove the burdens of your heart."

"You were born with potential. You were born with goodness and trust. You were born with ideals and dreams. You were born with greatness. You were born with wings. You were not meant for crawling, so don't. You have wings. Learn to use them to fly."

"God writes spiritual mysteries on our hearts where they wait silently for discovery."

"As you start to walk out on the way, the way appears."

"Always remember you are braver than you believe, stronger than you seem, smarter than you think and twice as beautiful as you'd ever imagined. Yesterday I was clever, so I wanted to change the world. Today I am wise, so I am changing myself."

I wish you well on your journey!

Made in United States
North Haven, CT
06 August 2024

55776043R00076